I hope you know
how many answered prayers
are contained in the two little words,
"Welcome home."
So glad you're home safe.

You.

You're the answer
to a prayer.
Me.
I'm blessed
to have you
in my life.

Praise God!

Am I right?

May the favor of
the Lord our God rest on us;
establish the work of our hands for us—
yes, establish the work of our hands.

Psalm 90:17 (NIV)

God gave us family

so we'd never forget

what love feels like.

So grateful for you.

You probably have no idea

what an answer to prayer you were.

May God be before you,
behind you,
beside you on your right and on your left,
above you and all around you,
everywhere you go today.

Based on St. Patrick's prayer

If only you knew how often

I whisper a prayer of thanks for you.

I can't thank God enough for you.

Or bacon . . . but you're definitely much better for my heart.

A blessing.

You.

Just calling it like I see it.

Thanks for your kindness—

you're an angel!

Got prayers?

Want some?

You're tops on my prayer list.

You even beat out calorie-free chocolate cake and faster Internet.

I feel a

HALLELUJAH

comin' on!

“The effectual, fervent prayer of a righteous person avails much . . .”

Well, there goes *my* plan.

Know what? I’m gonna pray anyway,

and trust Him. ’Cause it’s for a good cause. You.

God's got a plan.

And it's all good.

God cares.

I care, too.

I'm still thinking about you,

still keeping you in every prayer.

A prayer-a-chute never fails!

Lord, help me remember
that nothing is going to happen today
that You and I can't handle together.

Old Preacher's Prayer

You're at the top of
my prayer list—
somewhere between "world peace"
and "losing ten pounds."

Blessed are those
who expect nothing,
for they shall not be disappointed.

God is for you, and so am I.

Praying you will feel that today.

You are not alone.

God loves you.

And so do I.

I asked God to send you
an angel to encourage you.
Then I thought,
I can do that, too.
Not as much as an angel,
but I can pinch-hit.
Flying, not so much.

Encircled, protected, blessed . . .

that's you, every day, all day.

I'm adding a prayer benefit to your medical plan.

You're covered 24/7.

God is soooo good!

Amen?

DUCK!

Here comes a blessing.

I prayed for one to come your way,
and I have a feeling it's going to be BIG.

God loves you.

Just as you are.

Just be you . . .

the rest of us will sit back and say "wow."

May the Lord bless you—

big time!

These hands were made
for prayin'

and that's just what they'll do.

May the grace of the
Lord Jesus Christ,

and the love of God,
and the fellowship of the Holy Spirit
be with you . . .

2 Corinthians 13:14 (NIV)

Dear God,

Please make a way.
Open a window.
Kick in a door.
Blow the whole pop stand.
It would be so awesome.
Thanks.

He who watches over you will not slumber.

Psalm 121:3 (NIV)

Hear that? God is pulling all-nighters watching out for you!

Praying God helps you
look in a mirror
and see your own strength.
Then I'm praying He helps you
kick the kind of butt
we both know you can.

Dear God,

If it's Your will,
please make a way
for my sweet, wonderful friend.
And if it isn't Your will,
please give us both
a sense of humor about it
and the faith to keep asking,
because we will.

"Oops" happens.

So do miracles.

Just wait.

God has more than a few miracles
up His sleeve.
Praying for one with your name on it.

Rest, relax, be renewed . . .

you're in God's hands.

Praying for hope
that surprises you,

help that meets you where you are,
grace that finds its way in little by little.

“It is well with my soul.”

Praying that will be true for you today.

I told God everything

that's been going on with you.

He says it's under control.

Prayers Are Up; Worries Drop Off

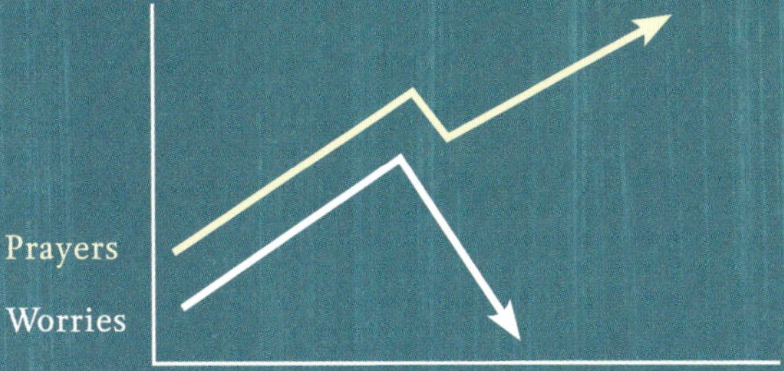

All this prayer should be paying dividends any minute now.

You're stronger than you know.

Praying for you and hoping you see
the strength in yourself that I do.

There are two things
you can always count on . . .
God's eternal love
and the love of your family.
We've got you surrounded.

The Lord is good to all.

Psalm 145:9 (NIV)

I don't know why we face hard times, but I do know it sucks.

Praying your life becomes less sucky soon.

I'm praying that you get just what you need for this day.

Plus a doughnut to boot.

I pray that you feel God's hand on your back gently guiding you.

And if it happens to lead you to have coffee with me . . . that's great, too.

The Lord bless you and keep you;
the Lord make his face shine on you
and be gracious to you;
the Lord turn his face toward you
and give you peace.

Numbers 6:24-26 (NIV)

Praying peace for you today.

A little sun to spill
into your world . . .
a little hope to ease into your heart . . .
that's what I'm praying for you.

Rest, relax, be reassured

you're in My hands.

Love, God

What better place could you be?

Dear God,

The stars?
Seriously—
awesome show.
So still, calm, and serene.
Please send that kind of peace and tranquility
to my friend.

OMGHISG

(Oh my God, He is so good!)

Praying you're surrounded by

quiet, peace, and serenity,

but most importantly . . . His love.

Grace and peace be with you.

May the Lord of peace himself

give you peace at all times

and in every way.

2 Thessalonians 3:16 (NIV)

I've been bugging the Big Guy

about sending you a break
and some good news soon.
And I'm going to keep it up, too.

Gonna be an AMEN kind of day!

This is the day that the Lord has made.

I hope it's also the day the Lord makes things turn around for you to stay!

Dear God,

Please smite whatever's bugging my bud
with Your Almighty Smiting Stuff.
Full Strength.
Thanks.

Hallelujah! Amen! Woo-hoo!

Good news like this
deserves some joyful noise!

Sometimes the answer is

"YES"

with three exclamation points!!!

God's got this.

God always comes through—

you're the perfect example.

Sit back,

relax,

and behold.

God's been orchestrating

these moments just for you . . .

how cool is that?!

Praying your day is full
of a thousand little miracles.

God always,

always

shows up.

I prayed for you today.

I'll pray for you tomorrow.
And I'll keep praying for you
as long as it takes.

Dear Father,

Asking for a miracle here.

A game-changer.

If it is Your will,

please knock it out of the park.

It would be so awesome.

Thanks.

Dear God,

Please point out the way
and smooth the road.
In fact, why don't You just drive for a while.
That would be awesome.

Fear not.

God is with you.

God's got your back.

And so do I.

I'm praying for you

to get back to 100%.

Because I 100% like you

and need you!

Prayer changes things.

And now you have the proof!

This calls for an

AMEN!

I don't envision cute angels.

I envision angels dressed
in battle gear ready for a fight.
And I see them with you now.

When you're fighting the good fight . . .

you can always use backup!

Prayers are with you.

You're facing some powerful stuff right now.

But prayer is even more powerful.
And it has been unleashed to kick butt
on your behalf.

That super-great,
on-top-of-the-world,
everything-is-awesome feeling
you're having right now?
Totally part of His plan.

Prayer goes a mighty long way.

I don't pray for dumb things like parking places.

I save it up for the big stuff.

This is big.

And so, I'm praying nonstop on your behalf—and trusting nonstop that God's listening.

Pray with expectation.

If you have enjoyed lifting others up
or these notes have touched your life in some way,
we would love to hear from you.

Please send your comments to:
Hallmark Book Feedback
P.O. Box 419034
Mail Drop 100
Kansas City, MO 64141

Or e-mail us at:
booknotes@hallmark.com